Clark Stanley

The Life and Adventures of the American Cow-Boy

Life in the far West

Clark Stanley

The Life and Adventures of the American Cow-Boy
Life in the far West

ISBN/EAN: 9783337208639

Printed in Europe, USA, Canada, Australia, Japan

Cover: Foto ©ninafisch / pixelio.de

More available books at **www.hansebooks.com**

INDEX.

The Life and Adventures of the American Cow-boy.
Cow-boy's Mountain Ranch.
Clark Stanley's Portrait.
Index.
Introduction.
Texas Steer.
Life in the Far West.
Driving Young Steers Up the Trail.
The Round-up.
Mavricks.
Cutting Out.
Cow Ponies.
Branding Calves.
Branding Cattle.
Water Routes.
How to Start in the Cattle Business.
How to Get 160 Acres of Government Land.
Settler's Rights.
Cow-boy's Outfit.
Cow-boy's Hat.

Long Hair.
The Big Handkerchief.
Buckskin Clothes.
Belt and Guns.
High Heeled Boots.
The Big Spurs.
The Heavy Saddles.
The Cow-boy.
My Last Trip Up the Trail.
Watching Cattle at Night.
Hunting and Trapping.
How to Tan Hides.
Advice to Hunters.
Prairie and Timber Wolves.
How to Become a Marksman.
Song of the Cow-boy.
Come to Texas.
Blazing Out the Way.
History of Clark Stanley.
The Prairie Dog.
History of Snakes.
Antidote for Snake Bites.

Introduction

IN presenting this book to the public, I have stated a great many facts which I am sure will prove very valuable and interesting to my readers.

So much has been said about the Western people, that a great many would at once form an idea that the West was not a good place for peaceable and lawabiding people to go to, but when you have carefully scrutinized the pages of this book you will at once take a different view. I have had enough experience in the Western country to know just exactly what I am saying, and I am giving this from actual experience among all classes, and I feel sure that this work will be the means of dispelling the false illusions of a large percentage of Eastern people in regards to the habits and customs of the so-called wild and wooly Westerner, and when you have carefully read the contents of this little book, you will have no fear of taking up your abode in the greatest and grandest country on the face of the GLOBE, the GREAT WEST.

Yours Respectfully,

CLARK STANLEY,

(Rattle Snake King.)

A TEXAS STEER

Life in the Far West.

SIXTY years ago, according to the geographers of that day, that vast stretch of country lying between the Missouri River and the Rocky Mountains, was an arid waste, useless for the purposes of mankind. To-day millions of cattle range the territory; and it is one of the most important sources of the world's food supply. These vast treeless plains, uninviting to the farmer, are the paradise of the ranchman.

The cattle barons own ranches as large as a New England State; thousands of smaller ranches occupy the fertile valleys, and the live stock interests of New Mexico, Wyoming, Montana, Texas and Colorado are of great value.

Life on the range,, though entailing hard work, is exhilarating in its freedom and out-door activity, as different as possible from the constraint of farm-work. Its excitement and freedom have great attractions for the adventurous; and the American "Cow-boy" with his sturdy broncho which he rides like a centaur, his Western saddle, his leather chaps, and his large sombrero will ride into history as a distinctively American product. The Texas steer with his wide-spreading horns was once the prevailing type. The breeds have been crossed with others, the result being a type with a large frame which fattens readily and makes good beef; and still retains the hardiness necessary to survive the hardships of winter. During the winter the cattle are not fed, but secure a scant subsistance from the dried bunch-grass, deep snows hide this, and thousands of cattle starve to death.

Small ranchers in the mountains cut hay to feed their cattle through the winter; but this is not done on large ranches, and starvation and freezing cause heavy losses to the large cattle raisers. The half wild cattle survive incredible hardships, and in the spring fatten with astonishing quickness. During the long winters, deep snows and fierce storms makes the ranchman a prisoner of the elements. With the melting of the snow, the idleness of the winter disappears, the ranch becomes a scene of excitement; and the Cow-boys, eager for change and activity, prepare for the exciting work that is before them. Then begins the varied life of the summer, which is one long camping trip, largely in the saddle, "riding the range," rounding up, "cutting-out," branding, etc. A round up is the great event of the year. Every owner has a brand of his own burned into the animals flank. This is a proof of ownership, and it is put on the calves while running with their mothers, which are identified by the brand. An unbranded calf separated from its mother is a maverick. Twice a year a round-up is held.

Thousands of cattle belonging to different owners are driven from all quarters to an appointed place, and by the most daring horsemanship, the cattle of the different owners are "cut out." There are cattle ranches as large as a New England State. Sometimes two hundred miles of wire fence mark the limits within which thousands of cattle bearing the owner's brand freely roam. Fences and cattle have enemies which the range rider must protect by constant watchfulness. The enclosure of great tracts of land is opposed by all but great cattle owners; and a wire fence is very apt to suffer from the exasparation of a defiant plainsman who must ride fifty miles around or else cut it, he generally cuts it, and as every man in the cattle country is prepared to defend his actions with his ever-ready six-shooter, the controversies between range-riders and fence cutters are exciting. A more serious duty of the range-rider is guarding the herds against "cattle thieves," an annoyance to owners of large herds and a constant menace to small ranchers. These desperadoes cause large losses to the former and complete ruin to the latter. Ruffins and desperadoes drawn from the worst elements of frontier life, reckless of danger, mocking at laws, they stop at no crime, and love the excitement of violence. They sometimes gather in gangs in some part of the cattle country where inhabitants are so few and so widely separated as to be helpless against the ready rifles of a dozen desperadoes, they sweep before them every bunch of cattle not safely corralled and guarded by a rifle. Many a rancher has seen his whole wealth of five hundred or more steers "rustled" before his eyes by men who claimed them as stolen from some other ranch ; with his rifle he defends his property deadly shots have replied, and the robbers passing on, have left behind them a dead man with a bullet in his heart. In his encounter with "rustlers" the range-rider risks his life and he risks it bravely and readily, for the justice of the plains, does not wait on the slow process of the law, but punishes the desperadoes on sight. For weeks and months the "Coy-boys" are in the saddle, riding accross country, over barren alkali deserts, through savage mountains and sleeping

COW BOYS AND COW PONIES

under the stars by night. Full of excitement and danger, the range rider's circuit, is nevertheless lonely, with no companion but his broncho, he sees no human being for days. At dark, he dismounts where a straggling group of cottonwoods, tells of water and grass.

As darkness fall and the stars shine out, his little campfire makes a point of light in the vast spaces of desert. A lonely meal, a half hour's smoke, and soon the dying glow of the fire, falls on a blanket wrapped, soundly sleeping form, with a pony silently grazing near by, while from the distance comes the wail of the cyote. Early in the fall comes a more social chapter in the cattleman's year. He joins his comrades and they gather the widely scattered herds from every part of the vast range. Not only one " brand," but many, are gathered when the ranges are not fenced. Each brand denotes a separate owner, and after the great annual " round-up," the thousands of cattle to be identified by different brands, are separated into different bunches. As far as the eye can see, the plain is alive with thousands of wild cattle, urged by hundreds of shouting men on their little ponies, all heading for the centre where the round-up is to be held. There are perhaps twenty thousand cattle gathered in a confused mass. Should they take alarm, become frantic and stampede, they will go for miles. The horsemen begin to circle about them ; round and round they go, the cattle crowd together and circle, likewise, and the impulse to run expends itself in " harmless " milling instead of a stampede.

Any one wishing information as to profits and losses in the cattle business as it is carried on at the present time, can find it or at least part of it in the following pages ; and also a few words of advice to those wishing to work on the broad cattle ranges of the West :

In Texas, not many years ago, the cost of raising a steer—was fifty cents, that being the cost of having him branded, when a calf. In those days men ran branding out-fits for the purpose of branding " mavricks " for themselves—and at the same time they would brand their poor neighbor's calves at fifty cents a head. In using the word poor, I mean men, not able to run a " branding out-fit " of their own. The men who conducted those " branding out-fits " used a forked pencil ; that is, when they branded a calf for a neighbor they would make a mark in their book, with this double-geared money maker. The consequence naturally was, that the poor man would have a double number of calves to pay for about New Years. But it turned out all right as in after years, the Eastern speculator went into the stock business with his eyes shut—that is, buying out whole brands of cattle according to the old books. For instance, if the aforesaid poor man could show up and prove that he had so many calves branded the PAST YEAR,—that is counting five head of cattle for every calf branded. Thus it will be seen that the forked pencil proved a blessing to the poor rancher. The day though, of inveigling the Eastern tenderfoot into paying for more than he really gets is past, never to return. The cost of raising a three year old steer on any of the large cattle ranges in the West, can be put down at $4.75 that is, when I was in the cattle business, as time glides on and the human feeling which now exists in the East shall invade the West, the cost will be more, as the building of sheds, etc. will be necessary for winter use.

To get that three year old steer in Chicago will cost $5.75 making the total cost, $10.50. The average weight of a three-year old Texas steer is 950 pounds, and the price per pound, putting it at the lowest, is three cents, making the steer bring $28.50, leaving a profit of $18.00

DRIVING YOUNG STEERS "UP THE TRAIL."

In South Western Texas, you can buy two-year-old steers for $10.00 a head, and to get them "up the trail" to any northern range will cost $1.00 a head to carry those steers over until the next shipping time, which is between June and October, will cost $2.00 more a head. Now add the cost of landing them in Chicago which I gave you above, add at the same time weight and prices as given above and you will have a profit of $9.75 a head. The losses by death, etc., are not included; you can safely put the losses "coming up the trail" at two per cent., providing you hire experienced men, and have good cow ponies, and the losses during the winter from deaths and other causes would be about one and a half per cent

THE ROUND-UP.

The round-up is an arrangement among the cattlemen in a given district to bunch the cattle. Each owner sends one or more Cow-boys to represent his brand and to take charge of all cattle that belong to his herd. The management is placed in the hands of an experienced man, and the ground to be covered is of great extent, occupying the men from one to six months. The main plan is to drive the cattle out of all outlying valleys into some central spot; out of the mixed bunch, the different brands are separated, beginning with the largest heards first. This is a great advantage to the large owners, as the object of the general round-up is to get at the young calves while they are being cut-out, as it is called, the cattle in the main hered are "churned" up, so that the calves get separated from their mothers; and as the only title to a calf is, that it is following a cow with your brand, those who cut-out last will certainly loose some which belong to them.

A COWBOY

"MAVERICKS."

All calves unbranded which are not following a cow are called "mavericks" and belong to the man on whose range they have been found.

"CUTTING-OUT."

The work of cutting-out a cow and calf is very pretty, one man can do it, but with two it can be done easier. The Cow-boy rides through the bunch of cattle until he sees a cow and a calf that belongs to him, he follows them quietly, trying to push them to the edge of the herd, when he gets them moving, he quickens his speed and when near the outside he will try to push them straight out of the bunch; but the cow does not like to leave her companions and tries by running round to break back into the main bunch, this the Cow-boy must prevent by riding between the cow and the main herd. Horse, cow and calf are soon running their best, and the Cow-boy must be ready to turn as quickly as the cow, he must be careful not to separate the calf, for should this happen his time is lost; he would then have to let the cow rejoin the herd and recover her calf. Each bunch of cows thus separated are kept at a distance. and are watched by a man to prevent them rejoining the main bunch. If the Cow-boy has been successful, the cow is soon tired out, and finding herself checked in doing what she wishes will stop; and seeing another bunch of cattle she will trot contentedly toward them, and having her calf with her will settle down quietly. This cutting-out goes on all day, until the whole herd has been separated. It is hard work on the men and also on the horses, which have to be changed three or four times during the day, the quick turning and stopping shakes them up, and brings on sore backs. Their mouths do no suffer much for the Cow-boy riding with a very severe bit has necessarily a very light hand and hardly uses the reins, the ponies know their work, and a touch on the neck brings them round at a pace which would send a new beginner out of his saddle.

THE COW PONIES.

The cow ponies are small animals, and half disappears under the heavy saddles of the Cow-boys, which often weigh from thirty-five to fifty pounds. The origin of the cow ponies is the broncho, which were first used in Texas, and they have been much improved in late years. The largest ponies are not always the best. A short pony of about fifteen hands works better than a larger animal. Each Cow-boy when out cow-punching, rides from five to eight ponies, using them in turns, riding one pony forty or fifty miles, of which a good deal may be fast riding.

After the day's work he takes off the saddle and bridle and lets the pony loose, who after a good roll rejoins the main herd of ponies. He will not be used again for several days. The cow ponies get nothing to eat but the grass they pick up. The heavy saddles are of great advantage as they distribute the weight of the rider and his kit over a large portion of the ponies back. In ropeing cattle the heavy saddle is necessary, there are two cinches; these must be well tightened, and even then the sudden jerks try the ponies severely. The end of the rope is held fast by a turn round the horn of the saddle which stands from five to seven inches above the pommel; the rider often hangs heavily over the further side of the pony to prevent the saddle being turned round.

BRANDING CALVES.

It is not necessary to have a corral to brand cattle in, but if you can run your bunch into one, it saves time and trouble. The corral is strongly made of posts and rails five feet high; just outside the corral a fire is lit, and one man keeps the branding irons hot, which he passes through the rails as they are called for. In a small corral, one Cow-boy on horseback is enough, unless there are many large calves to handle. A man with a lasso catches a calf by throwing it over his head. If it is a little calf he is dragged to one side, thrown down, cut and branded. To keep steadily at catching, throwing and branding is very hard work, and the Cow-boys will work at it very hard and through very long hours. To see the top man is a great sight, as he never tires running backward and forward between the fire and the calves, each time he puts on a brand he seals a piece of property worth ten to fifteen dollars. If branding is done in the open country, one man holds the bunch together, and the lassoer picks out the unbranded calves and drags them off to the fire.

BRANDING CATTLE.

To brand large cattle, you can do nothing without horses, the lasso must be thrown over the horns, and it takes two or three men to hold the animal after it is down. Throwing the large cattle does them more harm than good. One man should be able to catch, throw and brand a steer in the open country, but even with two or three men the object is not always accomplished so very quickly. If a man should dismount, the enraged steer would make for him, but sometimes in the changing and shifting the man on foot may get between the steer and the horse, the steer will make a rush at him and he is lucky if he escapes a tumble and a kick. When the cattle have been branded, the round-up moves on, the camp is broken up,

A ROUND UP

the wagons are packed and a string of four horse teams make a start. The Cow-boys with their leather chap and wide brimmed hats are riding off in different directions, and the place which was lively with bustle is left deserted marked only by the grass trampled down and the heaps of dirt round the old camp. The cyote will soon sneak in, and have his pickings on the scraps of leather, then all will be quiet till the round-up in the spring.

WATER ROUTES.

The trails usually chosen for travel across the plains furnish on an average, water every fifteen or twenty miles. In some instances, however, and during the dry season of the year it is necessary to go into what is termed "a dry camp."

HOW TO START IN THE CATTLE BUSINESS.

There is still room and wheather you wish to amuse yourself, or to try a new life, there are many openings; the only thing is to be carefull, settle and wait. To be on the safe side if you have money leave it at home; and learn the business by working at it with your own hands; hire yourself out; if active and willing you are worth your keep, and in two or three months if you are a sensible man and want to get on, your employer will be glad to give you wages, for good men are scarce, there are many that know their work but few will do it, and still fewer are to be trusted out of sight. You will soon be able to save some money—enough to make you think of investing; this will set you inquiring into prices of cattle and the chances of a return; you will probably make one or two bad deals and get some experiences and learn that saddest lesson—a distrust of men. After two or three years you may venture an independent start, you can take up 160 acres under the government land laws; or you may buy out some one who has a claim to sell suitable to your purposes; your money will help you to stock it and buy farm impliments.

HOW TO GET 160 ACRES OF GOVERNMENT LAND.

Any person who is twenty-one years of age and a citizen of the United States, and does not own more than 160 acres of land in any State of the United States can take up 160 acres of government land by stating that he is entitled to the land under the Homestead Act, and that he intends to settle on and cultivate it. The commission on 160 acres is $10.00. The settler must go and live on his claim within six months' from the time he makes the entry and reside there for five years, then he must furnish four witnesses that he has resided there for five years and also cultivated it. The United States government only allows one homestead to one person. A soldier having served in the rebellion ninety days or over can get 160 acres and have the time that he served in the army deducted therefrom, providing he served less than four years.

SETTLERS' RIGHTS.

There are, of course no absolute rights. The land is owned by the United States government. Some of the States have passed laws acknowledging settlers' rights on streams and pieces of land they have enclosed, but this is contrary to state law. Among stock raisers there is much give and take; the first settlers try to keep out new comers; but so long as there is grass, cattle will crowd in.

COW-BOY'S OUTFIT.

It is the general impression among the people of the East, that the long hair, wide-rimmed hats, big spurs, fringed leggins and other striking things in a Cow-boy's outfit are worn for show and bluster; but, like many other ideas about Cow-boys, that impression is entirely wrong. It was not a desire for picturesqueness that led to our make-up as it is to-day, questions of usefulness and necessity were the only considerations that prompted the adoption of our peculiar dress.

COW-BOY'S HAT.

Take, for instance, the Cow-boy's big-rimmed hat that has been worn without changing fashion for generation after generation is enough to indicate that use, not vanity, dictated its origin. Until recent years the Cow-boy made his own hats. A hole as near the shape and size of his head as he could make it was dug in the ground. A large round piece of raw hide, wet, soft and pliable was spread over the hole. With a bunch of grass the centre of the rawhide was pressed down into the hole until it assumed its size and shape. The surrounding circle of hide which was to be the rim was kept flat on the ground when the hat was moulded, it was left until it was dried by the sun, then it was taken to a place where smoke and heat scorched it so that it was water-proof, then it was trimmed with strings and was ready for use. When the sun is scorching hot, this great hat is much cooler than a straw hat. When the wind is blowing the sand in the Cow-boy's face he would suffer greatly, but for the protection afforded his eyes by the big-rimmed hat. When the mud is flying from the heels of stampeding cattle or the terrible hailstorms of the plains are pelting upon them, their hats are the best friends they have. Nowadays, the Cow-boy's hats are made in the East, and made of the best fur, of the best water

ROPING IN THE CORRAL

animals, they can wash them or soak them in water, after they have been exposed to all kinds of weather and they hold their shape as if they were just out of the factory, they will stand rough wear for many years. The Stetson hat is the most commonly used by the Cow-boys, they cost from $8.00 to $20.00, and if made to order they will cost a great deal more.

LONG HAIR.

As to long hair there are good reasons why the Cow-boy's wear it. Their business is out of doors, rain or shine and in many changes of climate, and they have found from experience that the greatest protection to the eyes and ears is long hair. Old miners and hunters know this well. Scouts, hunters, trailers and guides let their hair grow as a rule. Those who have been prejudiced against it have suffered the consequences of pains in the head, sore eyes and loud ringing noise in the ears. A result of exposure without the protection of long hair is loss of hearing of one ear, caused by one or the other of the ears being exposed more when the Cow-boy is lying on the ground. Healthy hearing and eyesight are of the greatest importance to the Cow-boy, scout or hunter. There are some white men whose interests call them to live among the Indians, and it is a fact that by letting their hair grow long they gain favor with the people they live among.

THE BIG HANDKERCHIEF.

I have heard people say that they should think the Cow-boy had enough things about him to attract attention without wearing a great big handkerchief about his neck instead of carrying it in his pocket, and yet if it wasn't for that handkerchief, the Cow-boy would frequently be put to much inconvenience, if not actual suffering. I have often had my face and eyes covered and filled with mud and sand while at full speed on my horse in a stampede or other danger. With my big handkerchief on my neck I have but to seize it and clean my eyes without stopping my horse's speed for a second as I would have to do if the handkerchief were carried in my pocket. It is very often called into use as a veil during the fierce sand storms the Cow-boy encounters in crossing the country. Being of great service in the sand storms, the Cow-boy cannot be too careful of the safety of his handkerchief; tied about his neck it is handy and secure. Many times when it is being used by the Cow-boy the stumbling of his horse at full speed will call into use both hands, and his handkerchief must be dropped instantly, there is no time to fumble for a pocket, and if it were not secured around his neck as it is, it would be lost.

BUCK-SKIN CLOTHES.

"Another thing that attracts the Eastern people is the fringed buck-skinclothing of the Cow-boy. 'Why don't they wear clothes like other people?' they say. The buck-skin leggings or—shaps as they call them—are worn by the Cow-boys to protect their clothes and limbs from the wear and tear of the heavy saddles, and also as protection against brushes with thorns, such as cactus, mesquite and many others.

BELT AND GUNS.

"The Cow-boy's belt, cartridges, open holsters and revolvers are not worn to scare people with; they wear them when crossing the country because it is necessary; they have large herds of cattle in their charge, and many times they have to cross hostile regions where there are horse thieves and other marauders; they keep well practiced in handling their guns; they can also do better shooting at long or short range with their heavy pistols than many soldiers can do with their rifles; they have them in open holsters all ready for use. There are times when they have to cripple cattle to save their horses in a stampede, and their pistols must be ready to their hand.

HIGH HEELED BOOTS.

"Then comes the boots. Many persons ask why the Cow-boys wear such high heels on their boots. We have our boots made to order, and they cost from $8.00 to $15.00 a pair; sometimes the tops are made stiff so they will not wrinkle. The heels on these boots are often two or four inches high, sloping greatly toward the sole of the foot, this is to keep their feet from slipping through the stirrup in times of danger; they are also kept in a comfortable position when riding.

THE BIG SPURS.

"The heavy, strong spurs that the Cow-boys use have been called curel; but, singular as it may seem, the light spurs used in the East are much more cruel, the heavy spurs serve a great purpose. Upon them the Cow-boy's life depends very often, many times their horses will not get up and out of the way of a wild steer dashing down upon him during a stampede unless he is severely spurred. If they had small rowels they could not reach the skin through the long hair and scurf nature provides the horses with to protect them from the severe winters of the plains. The spurs must be strong so that they will not break down in times of danger, and they don't want them to wear out before they reach their destination.

BRANDING CALVES IN THE CORRAL

THE HEAVY SADDLE.

"Many men say that they can't see why the Cow-boys use such large heavy saddles. Their saddles are not made for pleasure for they have to do heavy work with them, when they are ropeing cattle the saddle must be very strong and made of the very best of leather; they fix them on their horses so they will not be torn off while doing hard work; they use two cinches, one to keep the saddle from pitching forward when there is a steer on the end of the rope, the other one secures the saddle in the usual way, and they take particular care how they set them on the horse; they always have a heavy load to carry beside their own weight, but the burden is so distributed that it is easier on the horse than if they used one of the small short-horn saddles."

THE COW-BOY.

It may be well to give a reason for the name "Cow-boy," and how it first came into existence. History states that in the very earliest days of the arrival of civilization on this continent, the Spanish armies broke away and formed into bands of pirates and brigands. The loyal subjects which were principally missionaries, etc. were compelled to leave the gold country of the Montezumas—they were chased and hounded by the robbers. Some drifted North as far as Laramie and left a trail of adobe walls that will go down in the earliest history of this continent, such as Munchahambra, Pueblo, Santa Fee, El Paso, Del-Norte, etc., etc. Some drifted West and a few drifted East and settled in what is now known as San Antonio, Texas. This party of loyal people begged of Spain for help. Spain was then in great difficulties with other powers and the only thing she could do at this time to help her loyal subjects was to send cattle, horses, pigs, sheep and chickens. There were none of these domestic fowls and animals on this continent up to that time. The people then formed a new business and called themselves Vaquero's (meaning stock raisers). The business increased very rapidly and soon a market was found for hoofs, horns and hides in Europe, and in a short time many people from the Eastern settlements emigrated to Texas. The increase of the English speaking people alarmed Mexico. She who tried for many generations to compel the Texans to acknowledge themselves as Mexican subjects, but only to meet with defeat every time. The Texans kept themselves independent, but no nation would acknowledge their independence. Dear old Davie Crockett went to Washington several times but was only scoffed at and the politicians of the East made fun of his pleading. The Eastern politicians have changed but very little when there is a cry for protection from the West. In 1836, Santa Anna marched a large army across the Rio Grande into San

Antonio and killed all the Texans there with Davie Crockett at the old Fort Alimo. Then Sam Houston, Ben McCullah, Pat Cannon, Kit Karson and others of great fame as fighters against wrong, declared all of the people of Texas as members of the Texas army; men, women and children had to fight. Now they ask no help, but all alone, a single star on their flag, they bravely fought and were victorious, and the lone star compelled the world to acknowledge her a nation among nations until she was willingly admitted as one of the sister states of the union. The Texans now put their whole attention to the horse and cattle growing business, which was very profitable for hides, horns, hoofs, tallow and corned beef. The moneyed people of the states began to invest, and a great emigration from the States took place. The Spanish language which was entirely spoken, gave way to English, the word Vaquero lost its hold and the word Cow-boy took its place.

MY LAST TRIP UP THE TRAIL.

"It was in the Spring that I made my last trip up the trail with Mitchell's big herd, we started from the Rio Grande country on our long journey through Texas and the Indian Territory to Kansas. For months we had been rounding-up, branding and preparing for the trip, and finally all was ready and the herd was started North. Herds starting anywhere in Southern Texas must start early in the season, as it is an all summer drive if the cattle are to be brought through in good condition. Mitchell had in this herd five thousand long horns or Texas steers, mostly three-year-olds. The plan was to take them north well up in the Indian Territory, winter there, and push them into the market as early as they could be got into fit condition. The out-fit consisted of twelve men, besides a cook. Each of the twelve men were supplied with several ponies for riding; for on such drives frequent changes of horses are necessary. The cook was furnished with two pair of mules, a mess wagon for "chuck" or provisions, consisting principally of beans, coffee and flour, and a steer is always killed when needed on such expeditions. The drive had been on the road but five days and was hardly broken in—when just as night approached, a rain storm came up accompanied with wind, and at once the herd began to drift; that is, to work slowly ahead with the storm. The only thing to do when a herd begins drifting, is for the Cow-boys to keep with it, riding in front and at the sides; keeping it from breaking up into bunches and becoming separated. Cattle do not travel very fast in such cases, but they keep moving steadily with heads down, noses close to the ground, and any effort to stop them is likely to result in a stampede, and a

THROWING THE LARIAT

division of the drove into bunches, whereby it is likely to become mixed with other herds. When the storm came up, the men caught and mounted fresh ponies and resumed their places in the line which they had formed about the drifting herd endeavoring by the singing of songs and by keeping even pace with the cattle as they drifted to keep them from becoming uneasy and so hold them together.

But from some unknown cause the cattle stampeded. No one could tell what caused the stampede any more than one can tell the strange panics that attack human gatherings at times. A flash of lightning, a crackling stick, a wolf howl, little things in themselves, but in a moment every horned head was lifted and the mass of hair and horns, with fierce frightened eyes gleaming like thousands of emeralds was off, recklessly, blindly in whatever direction fancy led them, they went over a bluff or into a morass, it mattered not, and fleet were the horses that could keep abreast of the leaders; but some could do it, and, lashing their ponies to their best gait, the Cow-boys followed at breakneck speed. Getting on one side of the leaders the effort was to turn them a little at first, then more and more, until the circumference of a great circle was being described. The cattle behind blindly followed and soon the front and rear joined and "milling" commenced. Like a mighty mill-stone, round and round the bewildered creatures raced until they were wearied out or recovered from their fright. To stop the herd from "milling" was a necessary but difficult task. It was death to the animal that failed to keep up with its comrades, for in a moment his carcass would be flattened by thousands of trampling hoofs. The human voice was the most powerful influence that could be used to affect the brutes. As soon as the "milling" began the Cow-boys began to sing. It mattered not what, so long as there was music in it, and it was not uncommon to hear some profane and heartless bully doling out camp-meeting hymns to soothe the ruffled feelings of a herd of Texas steers. A stampede always meant a loss and rendered the herd more likely to be again panic-stricken. Often hysterical leaders were shot. Thus accompanied by incidents that brought into play all the strength and strategy of their guards the horned host moved on. Rivers were crossed by swimming in the same order that had been followed on land. Reaching the outskirts of the shipping station the herd was held on the plains until the drover effected a sale or secured cars for shipment. The animals were driven into the stockades, dragged or coaxed into the cars and were sent off to meet their fate in the great packing houses. But these days are things of the past. The great Texas ranches are enclosed with barbed wire fences, and a genuine Texas steer would attract almost as much attention in the old cattle towns as a llama. Ailbene, Newton and Dodge city are busy little cities surrounded by rich farming communities, and with churches, schools, electric lights and other evidences of modern civilization. No trace of the old life remains except some weather-stained and dilapidated buildings pointed out to the stranger as having been the saloon where Wild Tom, Texas Sam or other strangely named characters killed men unnumbered "during the old cattle days."

WATCHING THE CATTLE AT NIGHT.

I have been asked quite often, by people in the East, if the cattle have to be watched at night. The herd should never be left unwatched on the trail. When at night it is thought time they are driven to a bedding ground and bunched up, and when they have steadied down one or two men are left on watch, whose duty is to ride round and round the herd to prevent any straying. If the weather is not too cold and the cattle behave well this is not disagreeable work. The cool air is refreshing after the long day's heat; you walk your horse at a little distance from the cows; you must, however keep moving and show yourself on all sides. To hear the human voice seems to quiet the cattle, and the man on watch will often sing. One by one the animals lie down; the quiet of all these huge animals is impressive and seems in keeping with the sleeping earth and calm sky.

Provided nothing disturbs the peace, the cattle will lie still up to eleven or twelve o'clock at night, while you circle in the darkness round the black patch on the ground.

Before midnight, under some special ordinance of nature, the cows are restless and get on their feet; a few will try to feed out; these you must drive back again. But before that time, if you hold the first watch, you have probably been relieved and are back in your bed. Each man has a horse saddled and picketed near the camp all night; so if anything frightens the herd, or a storm comes on, all hands must turn out and mount. If the cattle have started you must be after them and bring them back to camp. Any one left behind will make a bonfire to direct the boys; but a dark night with rain prevents your seeing far, as the camp has often been chosen in a sheltered spot. The main thing is to keep the herd together if matters have been well managed and no serious disturbances have occurred. The herd makes up and starts out at daylight.

HUNTING AND TRAPPING.

Anyone can be a hunter and trapper; there is plenty of ground in the West that you can go on and hunt and trap, as it belongs to the U. S.

EXAMINING THE BRAND

Government, and no one will stop you if you don't destroy the timber. Of course it requires time and experience to be a good trapper, but one can soon learn and there are plenty of trappers you will come in contact with who will give you points, and plenty of them are Eastern people. It is no trouble to sell the furs to dealers.

But it all depends on the way the trapper skins them, as the more careful he is to not tear them, and also to stretch them out straight to dry and make them look good when he ships them, the more money he will get for them. A great many hunters and trappers case their skins, that is they don't cut them open on the belly, they start at the hind legs and turn the skin inside-out and then put them on a board to dry, and then they are called case skins, and some dealers prefer them and will pay more for them. The dealers grade the skins, and they are called number one, number two, number three and number four; the number one's are the best and bring the most money.

TO TAN HIDES.

Take two-thirds of pulverized alum and one-third fine table salt, mix together, wet the inside of the skin and let it remain twenty-four to twenty-eight hours; scrape off the loose flesh, apply the alum and salt the second time and rub in until it becomes soft, dry in the shade; this is the way hunters tan hides for their own use. Very few hunters do any tanning for the market as they generally ship the skins to the dealers after they are dried, then they are called raw.

ADVICE TO HUNTERS.

Never be in a hurry, don't get excited when you go hunting, take things cool and don't shoot until you are sure you are close enough; there is just as much in knowing how to decoy game as there is in being a good marksman, and always keep on the look-out when you are in a piece of timber, lest some animal might spring on you from ambush.

The most dangerous animal in the West is the mountain lion; you sometimes come right up to within ten or twelve feet of him, where he lies crouched like a huge dog, then the only way is to back off slowly, and at the same time keep your eye on him; when you are about twenty feet away you can raise your rifle and shoot, but should you wound him you must prepare for a fierce fight, for he will instantly spring on you, and once in his claws, you might as well say your prayers, but if you can get your hunting knife in his breast then you are all right. Never turn your back to a mountain lion, always walk off backwards, and very slowly too, so as not to excite him. The wild cat is also a dangerous customer to deal with ; always when you shoot one be sure he is dead before you try to pick him up, for if he is not he will turn on you and scratch you.

PRAIRIE AND TIMBER WOLF.

The best time to kill the timber wolf is in December, January and February; then they have a full coat of fur. There is a great deal to learn to be a professional trapper. The fox is one of the slyest animals to trap as they are very suspicious, and if you set a trap for them you must not disturb the ground much where you set your trap; leave everything as near the way you find it as when you go there. The prairie wolf is known as the biggest coward in the West; you can chase a pack of fifty of them with a little black and tan dog, but as soon as the dog stops chasing them, they will in turn chase the dog as long as he runs from them, but as soon as he stops and makes a bluff at them again, the whole pack will start and run from him again. It is great fun to look on and see it.

The timber wolf is much larger than the prairie wolf, they don't bluff so easy; a pack of ten of them could make it very warm for that many large dogs. They can kill cattle, sheep and human beings. My advice to tenderfeet is not to take any chances with them. There is a bounty paid on the scalps of prairie and timber wolves by the different Western States.

HOW TO BECOME A MARKSMAN.

Stand straight up, and when shooting in a gallery never lay down on the counter to rest your arm, for if you once get into that habit it is hard to break off. Stand erect, and place your right foot six inches behind the left foot, with the hollow of the right foot opposite the left heel; in taking aim, be as quick as possible, catch the sight as soon as you can, for the longer you hold the gun to your shoulder trying to get better aim, the more shaky your nerves will get, and your eye may become watery. The first sight is always the best, as shooting is nothing more or less than good eyesight and steady nerves.

To do fine fancy shooting with the aid of a looking-glass, stand your back towards the target, place the rifle on your right shoulder so that it will balance, grasp the small of the stock with your right hand, the thumb on the trigger, place the glass in the left hand, and between the thumb and fore-finger, rest the hand on the stock of the rifle between the butt and the small of the stock, look in the glass and keep moving until you get the muzzle and rear sight on a line just the same as shooting from the shoulder, it may take some time and patience at first, but when you once get the idea it is dead easy; other shots may be done the same way, namely, on top of head, over left arm, between the legs, etc.

MESS WAGON—MORNING MEAL

SONG OF THE COW-BOY.

Come, give me your attention,
   And see the right and wrong,
It is a simple story
   And won't detain you long;
I'll try to tell the reason
   Why we are bound to roam,
And why we are so friendless
   And never have a home.

My home is in the saddle,
   Upon a pony's back,
I am a roving Cow-boy
   And find the hostile track;
They say I am a sure shot,
   And danger, I never knew;
But I have often heard the story,
   That now I'll tell to you.

In eighteen hundred and sixty-three,
   A little emigrant band
Was massacred by Indians,
   Bound West by overland;
They scalped our noble soldiers,
   And the emigrants had to die,
And the only living captives
   Were two small girls and I.

I was rescued from the Indians
   By a brave and noble man,
Who trailed the thieving Indians,
   And fought them hand to hand;
He was noted for his bravery
   While on an enemy's track;
He has a noble history
   And his name is Texas Jack.

Old Jack could tell a story
   If he was only here,
Of the trouble and the hardships
   Of the Western pioneer;
He would tell you how the mothers
   And comrades lost their lives,
And how the noble fathers
   Were scalped before our eyes.

I was raised among the Cow-boys,
   My saddle is my home,
And I'll always be a Cow-boy
   No difference where I roam;
And like our noble heroes
   My help I volunteer,
And try to be of service
   To the Western pioneer.

I am a roving Cow-boy,
   I've worked upon the trail,
I've shot the shaggy Buffalo
   And heard the coyote's wail;
I have slept upon my saddle,
   And covered by the moon;
I expect to keep it up, dear friends,
   Until I meet my doom.

COME TO TEXAS.

The "Lone Star" is waving—the flag of the free—
Then strike for Texas, if men you would be;
No idlers are wanted, the thrifty and wise
To wealth and high station can equally rise.

Were corn, oats and cotton; the richest of loam,
Which yields to the settlers provisions and home.
Trees of every description arise on each hand,
From alluvial soil to rich table land.

Here springs are exhaustless and streams never dry,
In the season from winter to autumn's bright sky.
A wide panorama of prairie is seen;
Of grasses of all kinds perennially green.

Here millions of cattle, sheep, horses and goats
Grow fat as if stall-fed or fattened on oats.
No poverty is found in the mighty domain,
To the man who exerts either finger or brain.

Here are homes for the millions, the rich and the poor,
While Texas opens wide her hospitable door,
She has thousands of acres—yes, millions—to sell,
Yet can point without cost to where pre-emptors can dwell.
Her terms will be easy with those whom she deals,
While security all in their title can feel.

Buy land while 'tis cheap, and the finest select,
'Twill, young men, prove a fortune when least you expect.
Old man, for your children, buy, file it away;
A Godsend 'twill prove on some rainy day.

When speaking of Texas, it must be borne in mind that an expanse of country, 825 miles long and 740 miles wide, containing an area of 252,514 square miles. It is a territory larger than all the New England States combined, and greater in area than any two States situated east of the Mississippi River. Compared to the countries of Europe, it has 34,000 square miles more than the Austrian Empire, 62,000 more than the German Empire, and nearly 70,000 square miles more than France.

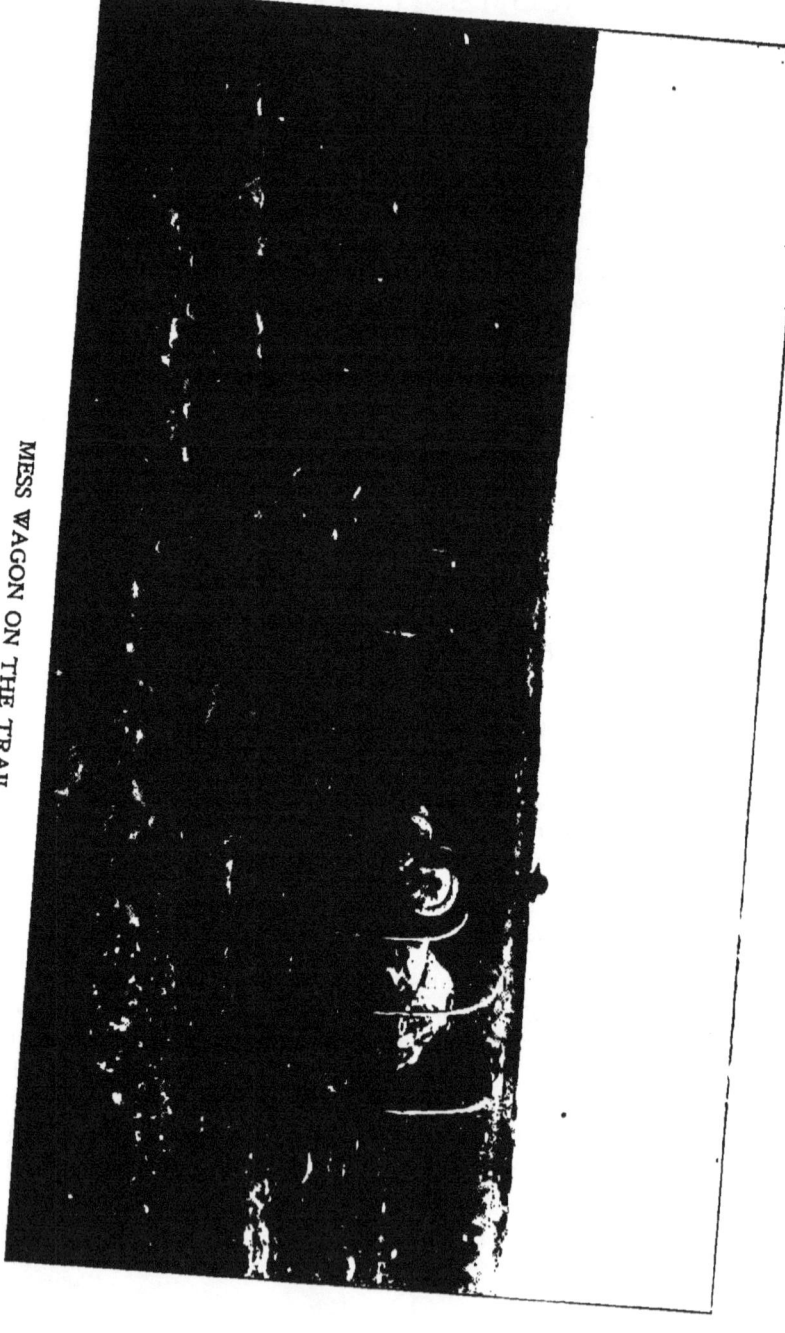

MESS WAGON ON THE TRAIL

BLAZING OUT THE WAY.

(COMMUNICATED.)

The men came on surveying
  And reached the Texas line,
Where summer breezes swept the plains
  With music half divine.

And there the people said to them,
  "We know not why, nor how,
But this we know, these valleys rich,
  Will never do to plow."

And thus the people argued,
  In manner weired and strange,
About these fertile valleys, fit
  For naught but cattle range.

That they were good for grazing
  Was plainly to be seen,
If you would take for evidence
  The grasses soft and green.

Where many thousand cattle fed,
  Contented on the plains,
Where "Madame Rumor" had it, that
  "It never, never rains?"

And thus the railroad men replied,
  "A desert, do you say!"
But while they spoke, they onward marched,
  Still blazing out the way.

"We are fond of deserts, such as this
  That now before us lies,
With singing birds and rippling streams,
  And cloudless summer skies.

"And here we think we can explain,
  Can tell the 'why and how,'
Just now the cattle man is king,
  And fears the farmers' plow.

"So he sends fourth these rumors wild,
  About the fearful draught,
That he in quiet may remain
  King of this Sunny South."

And as they onward pushed their work,
  The people all would say,
That money put in railroads here
  Was simply thrown away.

But still these men pushed forward
  Across the sunny land,
And built the grand old T. and P.
  Out to the Rio Grande.

Then farmers came upon the scene
  And settled down to stay,
And grew vast crops of cotton, corn,
  And wheat, and oats, and hay.

Then towns sprang up along the line
  And into cities grew,
And everything was "push" and vim
  Within this country new.

And much from forest and from mine
  Was added to our wealth,
And invalids from Northern climes
  Were soon restored to health.

Then other roads looked on and saw
  The products of the State,
And said "we, too, will enter now,
  Before it is too late."

And thus they came upon the scene,
  Plunged forth into the fray;
But still the grand old T. and P.
  Is blazing out the way.

[J. P. B.

I was born in Abilene, Taylor County, Texas, and at the age of fourteen I took my first trip up the trail and followed the life of a Cow-boy for eleven years. After the "round-up" in the Spring of 1879 I started with some of my father's best friends to the Moki, Pueblos at Wolpi, Arizona, to witness the snake dance which takes place once in two years; there I became acquainted with the medicine man of the Moki tribe, and as he liked the looks of my Colt's revolver and asked me to show him how it would shoot, I gave him an exhibition of my fancy shooting, which pleased him very much; he then asked me how I would like to stay there and live with him, I told him I would stay until after the snake dance. After my friends and I witnessed the snake dance, they returned to Texas, and I was so much pleased with the dance I decided to remain with them and see the dance again. I lived with the Moki tribe two years and five months, and during that time I learned their language and dances and the secret of making their medicines. The medicine that interested me most, was their Snake Oil Medicine as they call it. It is used for rheumatism, contracted cords and all aches and pains. As I was thought a great deal of by the medicine man he gave me the secret of making the Snake Oil Medicine, which is now named Clark Stanley's Snake Oil Liniment. Snake Oil is not a new discovery, it has been in use by the Moki's and other Indian tribes for many generations, and I have made an improvement on the original formula.

After leaving the Moki Indians I went to my home in Texas and seeing some of my friends there who were troubled with rheumatism I concluded to make my first Snake Oil Liniment and I gave several bottles away to my friends, and it proved such a success in curing them that I began to manufacture it and put it on the market, I traveled through the Western and Southwestern States and met with unbounded success, and during the World's Fair in Chicago in 1893, as an advertisement I made my Snake Oil Liniment in full view of the audience, killing hundreds of snakes which were shipped to me by my two brothers from my home in Texas. While doing business in Chicago, I got acquainted with many druggists from different parts of the United States.

A druggist from Boston who attended the World's Fair and witnessed my killing of the snakes and the manufacturing of the liniment became deeply interested, and through him I was induced to come East and I settled in the town of Beverly, Massachusetts, nineteen miles from Boston on the Boston and Maine railroad. There I started to manufacture Snake Oil Liniment for the eastern trade; finding my factory too small I decided to go to Providence, R. I. where I secured a plant much more suitable for my business, where I am now permanently located.

ROUND-UP DRIVING

What the Boston Transcript has to say about CLARK STANLEY keeping rattlesnakes for pets:

Down in Beverly, at No. 67 Park street, there is a man who has some of the most singular pets in the world. To this strange man's abode the writer made his way a few days ago, and upon stating his mission was immediately conducted to Mr. Stanley's sanctum. These pets are rattlesnakes, and he takes great care of them; but, so far as the fear of anyone's stealing them goes, there is not the slightest need of it, for the pets are nothing less than snakes of the most venomous species, they are in full possession of all their poisonous qualities; yet their owner fondles them and handles them as if they were stuffed; he keeps them in his bed-room in a large box, but has not the slightest fear of sleeping there with them as he knows they would never touch him. He is a manufacturer of Snake Oil Liniment, and he uses snakes in the manufacture of the oil. Several of them he keeps as pets and says that he would not sell them for a thousand dollars each if he could not replace them with others as good. These, however, although not made into oil, will be used in his business, as he gives exhibitions with snakes for the purpose of selling his liniment.

About the first of April he will get in a fresh invoice of snakes from his home in Texas. When the snakes arrive in Beverly, the manufacturer picks out the most "intelligent" for exhibition purposes. As soon as the snakes are well trained the family goes on the road to sell the liniment. On stopping at a town they first give an exhibition with the snakes, which generally draws about everyone who is able to get out of doors. He then takes one of the snakes, which is not susceptible of training, and delivers a lecture on the character and habits of the snakes. He kills the creature with cloriform, cuts it open, and shows where the fat lies, explaining how the fat is made into oil and the oil into liniment. Then he sells the liniment. Besides the sale of the liniment, he tans the skins and makes them into slippers, belts and neckties, and sells the rattles to be put in violins in order to keep the insects out.

The Transcript reporter saw the pet snakes at Beverly and can vouch for the fact that they are genuine creatures, and not those elusive visions which come from toying too freely with strong waters. The snake man took the reporter up to his bedroom, and opening a light wooden box, with a wire window in the side, dove his hand into it with as much unconcern as if he were taking an egg out of a basket, and brought it out again with a snake seven feet long writhing in it. "This," he said, as he hung the fearful creature round his neck, "is a Mountain Rattlesnake" and are found from Maine to Arkansas and Texas, and is the most deadly snake in this country, if not in the world. "This," another dive and another snake not so large "is a copperhead, which is next in venom to a rattlesnake, and this," he concluded proudly, bringing out a snake larger than either of the other two, "is a diamond back rattlesnake, from Rock Ledge, Florida." The creatures twined themselves about his body, poking under his clothing, and finally all three reared up their heads against his face, rubbing against it, and running their forked black tongues in and out against his flesh.

"The bite of any one of these snakes," he went on, "is absolutely deadly. No, their fangs are not drawn, I'll show you that." He caught one of the snakes by the neck and forced open its mouth, using apparently all the strength of his strong hands to do so. There sure enough were the deadly little curved fangs, white as milk, and sharp as needles laid back against the roof of its mouth. "Now when they strike," said the snake-man, "they erect those fangs, strike them into the flesh, and then draw back, injecting the poison through them as they do so. No," he answered in reply to a perfectly natural question, " I am not in the least afraid of being bitten. In fact, I have been bitten hundreds of times. Look here!" he went on, holding out his hands. They were covered as far up as the wrists with little white scars. " Everyone of those " he said, " is a snake-bite, some of them are poisonous, some not. When I go to work to train a snake I take a little rubber ball and hold it out to him, stirring him up so that he strikes at it again and again, until all the poison in his glands is exhausted, when he becomes harmless. Then I take the ball and bury it deep, for it is filled with poison. There is not the slightest use in extracting a snake's fangs, for there is no kind of snake which will not grow a new fang in forty-eight hours ; the rattlers grow them in thirty-six.

" I have been bitten many times by snakes with their poison drawn in this way, which of course is only temporary, as they soon fill the gland with poison again, but I have also been bitten by snakes which had their glands full of poison, and meant business of the most business like sort. The reason that I am not dead is because I have what I believe is the only remedy for snake-bite, and there is no question that it is a perfect one.

" Snakes," said the snake man, are like other animals. If you are not afraid of them, they are not afraid of you, and sometimes they will follow you a little way, though this is very rare. But if you show that you are not afraid, after you have mastered them once or twice, they will fear you, and you can do anything you like with them, short of really hurting them, and they will never harm you. They will always know you, too, after they have once gotten used to you. Now, you may have noticed when I first put these fellows round my neck, they ran their heads all over my coat, and then up against my face. The reason of that was that they

tell you by the smell, and there was a smell on this coat that they did not know about. I had spilled some of the liniment on it while I was working, and I should have changed it before I took them out, but I forgot about it. When they smelled the liniment, they did not quite know what to make of it, so they ran their heads up and smelled of my face, and then they knew that I was all right. I was not quite sure about that Diamond Back Rattler, I thought at one time that he was going to strike me. Now, if I should put them on you, they would strike you quicker than lightning, because they do not know you." He was not pressed for any demonstration of this statement.

It might be thought that the neighbors would object to having snakes about in this free-and-easy manner, but they do not, for two reasons; the first being that there are only a few neighbors in that vicinity, and the other that these few do not know that the snakes are there. When the new consignment comes from Texas, it may be different. There are only one or two people in Beverly, in fact, who know that the snakes are kept by this man. One of these is a driver for the Adams Express Company, and he is not likely to forget it in a hurry. The snake man tells the story of this expressman's introduction to the snake business with a good deal of relish. "He brought me a big rattler in a box," he says. "It was a wire box, so that he could hear and see what was in it, and when he came up the stairs he had one finger on each corner of the box, and was holding it off from him at arm's length. He set the box down on the floor, and had no more than set it down when I had the cover off. When you let out a rattler, the first thing he does is to rear up on end and look round to see where he is. Well, that's the way this one did. As soon as the cover was off the box, he shot up into the air about three feet, and began to work his head round and round in a circle. Well, sir, that expressman let out a whoop that you could hear for three blocks, and went down the stairs eight steps at a time. He never came round after his money until two days afterward, and then he just put his head inside the down-stairs door, and nothing could get him any closer to the rattler than that."—Boston Transcript.

THE SNAKE MAN OF BEVERLY.

Snakes with fangs, and snakes without fangs ; snakes poisonous, and snakes harmless; snakes long and snakes short—wriggling glossy reptiles—numerous and creepy enough to drive a teetaler into the "jim-jams," and afford a glimpse of the bottomless pit to the drunkard.

Such are the creatures that abound at No. 67 Park street, Beverly, the home of Clark Stanley, the trainer and handler of these reptiles, whose ancestors were forbidden in the dawn of the world's history to relinquish forever the luxury of leg locomotion, and commanded to crawl, instead, upon their bellies.

To this strange man's home the writer called a few days ago, and was immediately conducted to Mr. Stanley's office. When I entered Mr. Stanley was the sole visible occupant, and he greeted me cordially.

Immediately following mutual introduction the conversation turned upon snakes a subject in which the host soon proved himself perfectly at home.

After a somewhat lengthy dissertation about the many different species of reptiles, I interrupted him with the question :

"Have you any live snakes now in your possession?"

"Several," was the prompt answer.

Then to my amazement and horror he opened a box and took out two large rattle snakes.

"These are my especial pets" exclaimed Mr. Stanley.

"Are you not afraid of being bitten?" I inquired in awe-stricken tones from my vantage seat behind a sofa.

"Not in the slightest." I have been bitten by snakes time and again, with their glands full of poison. The reason I am not dead is because I have a cure for snake-bite, and I have never known it to fail.

"Snakes," continued Mr. Stanley, "are like other animals." If you are not afraid of them they are not afraid of you. If you shrink from them, they will strike at you, and sometimes pursue a man. But, if one shows himself not afraid, they are mastered, and will subject themselves to any treatment short of injury.

"Yes, I've been bitten hundreds of times. Look here!" holding out his hands, which were covered far up at the wrists with little white scars. "Everyone of those is a snake-bite, some poisonous, some not."

"There is not the lightest use in extracting a snake's fangs, for no snake exists which will not grow a new fang in forty-eight hours. Why, the rattlers produce a brand new fang in thirty-six hours."

Mr. Stanley has among his collection several species of snakes which he has for exhibition purposes, all under six feet in length, which he only feeds once in every six weeks, but gives water every day.

"Have you any other snakes?" I asked, Mr. Stanley. "Certainly."

"May I see them?" I asked, as I emerged from the protection of the sofa.

The lid of a box was opened and I gazed, with my hair standing on end "like quills upon the fretful porcupine."

There lay a knotted mass of snakes, the bodies **coiled around about** each other. The largest was of a yellowish color, with black marks shaped like the letter V extending the full length of their backs, irregular spots on the sides, very small neck, large head and almost black tails with the rattles jointed on the ends of them.

The Beverly police have considered it their duty to examine the premises of Clark Stanley, and are prepared to assure the neighbors that none of the snakes can escape from the house on Park street.—Boston Sunday Post, March 15, 1896. R. J. G.

A MAN WHO DOES NOT FEAR SNAKES.

Clark Stanley fondles and caresses poisonous reptiles without dread.

Clark Stanley, who is at present located at 21 Broad street, giving lectures on snakes and their habits, seems to have wonderful control over the poisonous reptiles, in fact, he has several which are pets. He has no dread or fear of any of the venomous species and handles and fondles them as if they were stuffed. He is the owner of several trained snakes which he exhibits while on the road selling his Snake Oil Liniment.

This week a Post reporter called upon Clark Stanley who exhibited several of his pets. The creatures entwined themselves around his body, and finally rubbed their heads against his face, at the same time running their forked tongues against his flesh. He said in reference to a rattlesnake; the bite of this species is absolutely deadly.—Sunday Post, Pawtucket R. I.

History of Snakes.

ALTHOUGH the history of snakes is as old as the history of the world, still there is probably no living creature that creeps on the face of the earth, that the people in general know less about than they do of snakes and their habits.

It is a very mistaken idea that snakes are all poisonous, dirty, filthy, horrible, devilish, ugly creatures, for they are not. There are but very few species of snakes that are poisonous or venomous. There is no creature cleaner in their habits than a snake. They always keep themselves clean, and will eat nothing except what they kill themselves. They are beautiful in color, graceful in every movement, intelligent and very friendly to all who are friendly to them; but they remind me of a looking glass. And as I notice hundreds of people looking into a snake den and making different remarks. I can tell very close the disposition of the person by their opinion of the snake.

What do snakes eat?

This question is asked probably more than any other. Each specie has its own favorite food. All species eat living creatures, and no specie chews their food, but swallows everything whole. All species of venomous snakes, such as the rattle-snake, copper-head, cotton-mouth, etc., kill their prey, which consist of rabbits, squirrels, mice, etc., with their own poison. All species of climbing snakes, such as the black-snake, chicken-snake, king-snake, etc., kill their prey; which consists of birds, squirrels, bats, etc., by their squeezing power. All species of low land or swamp snakes, such as the moccasin, spread-head, garter-snake, etc., swallow their prey, which consists of toads, frogs, fish, etc., without killing it in any way. Once in four weeks is often enough for any snake to eat; providing, they get enough at each feeding, but they should have water oftener. The life of a snake is about the same as that of man.

THE MOUNTAIN RATTLE-SNAKE.

The Mountain Rattler, as he is usually called, is the largest specie of rattle-snakes in the world, they are found wild in the hills and mountains of America, and America only, and are usually of a yellowish color, with black marks shaped like the letter V, extending the full length of the back, and irregular spots on the sides, very small neck with large head and body; the tail is almost black and the rattles joined on the end of it. Each joint of the rattle denotes one year of the snake's age; each year they add one new joint to their rattle. This does not, however, come on the end of the rattle, as a great many suppose, but it grows in between the end of the snake's tail and rattle. The first joint that they have which appears when the snake is one year old, always remains at the end of the rattle, unless broken off, in which case it will never grow again. This first joint is usually called the button.

All of the poison found about one of these snakes is in the head, and is known as venom. On each side of the upper jaw is a poison tooth. These fangs are shaped like a cat's claw, and being hollow the venom passes through them and is instantly injected into whatever the snake may strike. These fangs are on a hinge and remain folded up in the upper jaw when not in use. Besides these poison teeth they have one row of very fine teeth on both sides of each jaw, which are not poisonous in the least, and are used only to aid them in swallowing food, as each one of these little teeth points slightly back towards the throat which prevents anything which the snake tries to swallow from coming back out of its mouth. Their principal food is rabbits and squirrels which they kill by their own poison and swallow whole. They usually eat about every six weeks, and after eating their fill, they crawl away, coil up and lie there for the food to digest, which requires from seven to fourteen days. During this time the outer skin dries all over the body, over the eyes as well as the other parts, and this it is which causes the snake to go blind for a short time. I wish to call special attention to the fact that "dog days" has nothing whatever to do with any species of snakes going blind. After this outer skin is entirely dead a slime will form between it and the new one, providing the snake is on the ground where it can obtain moisture, he will then rub his nose until the skin breaks away at the nose, and keep rubbing it back towards the eyes. As soon as this passes the eyes he can again see as well as ever, he will then crawl out of the old skin which will leave him bright and pretty. They as well as all other species of snake never close their eyes, although this snake is very dangerous, there is no species more honorable than he is. He seems to realize his power and will never use it except in a case of necessity or self defence. These snakes get very fat in the summer season, and for many years the Indians and Mexicans have made a practice of rendering out the oil, which they pronounce a great remedy for the cure of rheumatism, deafness, contracted muscles, etc.

THE TIMBER RATTLE-SNAKE.

The timber rattle-snake is next to the mountain rattler in size, and also resembles it in form and habits, but they are usually of a greyish color and are always found in the timber, spending the summers in the low lands and going into the high lands for winter quarters, where they den up in large numbers in holes in the ground or crevices in the rocks. These places are called dens, and are occupied by the same family of snakes from one generation to another. After the last cold spell is over, in the spring they crawl out and leave the den in pairs, each pair taking a different direction in search of food, often going ten or twelve miles from the den to which they do not return until fall. They breed but once a year, having from four to eight young ones at a time. The young ones always remain with the mother, and should danger approach she will open her mouth and at a certain signal the young ones will all run down her throat for safety. These young snakes are never seen to eat anything the first season of their life, although they grow very rapidly, and it is my opinion that they gain nourishment by some means after being swallowed by their mother. This is also the case with several other species of snakes.

The fangs of the timber rattle-snake are constructed the same as those of any other venomous snake. The age of these snakes is about the same as that of man; they undoubtedly live to be over one hundred years old; but, of course, in that length of time they lose more or less of their rattles and their age can only be judged by the width of their rattles and not by their number, as each new joint is a little wider than the one preceding it—the older the snake, the wider the rattle.

These snakes have become of late years quite a benefit to man, as their skins are manufactured into fancy belts, slippers, neckties, hatbands, etc. The rattles are used in the violin to improve the tone of the instrument as well as to keep out insects; they are also worn in the hat to prevent headache, and their oil the same as all other species of rattle-snakes is used for the cure of rheumatism, contracted muscles, stiff joints, deafness, etc. The backbone is also used for making Indian beads.

The eyes of these snakes are the color of their bodies, and at first sight one would judge them to be blind. These snakes eat nothing in winter while they are in the den, but gain nourishment from the fat on their bodies which they accumulate during the summer; their food is the same as that of any other species of venomous snakes; they live almost entirely on small animals which they swallow whole.

THE DIAMOND-RATTLER.

The diamond-rattler is the prettiest of the rattle-snake tribe. They are marked with three rows of silver grey diamonds the full length of the back.

THE COPPER-HEAD.

The copper-head, like the rattle-snake is deadly poison; and the shape of the body is the same as that of the rattler, they are found in different shades of color, varying from a light pink to a dark copper color.

THE COTTON-MOUTH.

The cotton-mouths are found only on low ground. Shape of body same as rattler. Color, dark muddy, inside of mouth white as snow.

THE BULL-SNAKE.

This snake is known by several different names. He is called the bull-snake because he sometimes makes a noise resembling that of a bull; he is called the cow-snake because he sometimes sucks cows; he is called milk-snake for the same reason; he is called the blow-snake for the reason that when he is frightened he blows, making a loud noise; he is called the North American Anaconda, as he resembles them in appearance and habits.

These snakes are found in nearly all parts of North and South America. They are the largest species found in British America, and the farther South, the larger they are found to be.

In the tropical regions of South America they get to be monstrous, they are spotted black and yellow. These snakes kill their food by coiling around it and crushing it, and as soon as it is dead they cover it with a saliva and swallow it whole. They eat about every four weeks, then go blind and shed their skins. A bull-snake measuring five feet in length will swallow from four to ten rats at a time. They lay eggs but once a year, laying from ten to twenty at a time which it requires them less than three day's time to accomplish. Their eggs are about the size of pigeon's eggs, but are very long, large in the center and tapering down small at each end, and the same as all snake's eggs are, soft shelled.

THE BLACK-SNAKE.

The black-snake is found in timbered countries, black as jet all over, excepting under jaw, which is white.

THE CHICKEN-SNAKE.

The chicken-snake is the same as black-snake, but marked with dim diamond-shaped marks all over the body.

THE KING-SNAKE.

The king-snake is a very pretty snake, speckled green and black all over body. They can whip almost any other specie and often eat them.

THE PILOT-SNAKE.

The pilot-snake is a very glossy snake, marked the same as a Massoger Rattler, with round brown spots over a greyish back ground.

THE SPREAD-HEAD.

The spread-head-snake, sometimes called Adder or Viper, is found in three different colors, brown, black or spotted. When frightened they spread themselves flat, and when hurt they usually bite themselves and play dead which give people the idea that they are very poisonous, but they are not venomous in the least.

THE RING-NECK.

The Ring-neck is a small specie of snake with a bright ring around the neck.

THE BLUE-RACER.

The Blue-racer is blue all over and a fast runner.

THE GREEN-SNAKE.

The green-snake is green all over and never gets very large, and is nearly always found in the top of a bush.

THE WATER MOCCASIN.

There are a great many species of these snakes, such as the crossback, the mud, the wood-house, the black, the stump-tail, etc., but they all stay around the water and spend their lives as fishermen.

THE COPPER-BELLY.

The Copper-belly is of a slate color excepting the belly which is of a copper color.

THE GARTER-SNAKE.

The garter-snake is the most common snake in America, found mostly along creeks; striped red, black and yellow.

THE JOINT-SNAKE.

The joint-snake, sometimes called the glass-snake. In appearance is like a piece of glass; and when hurt, his tail, which is three times as long as his body will break into pieces. These pieces will never join themselves together again, but a new tail will grow out.

THE COACH-WHIP.

The Coach-whip is very long and slim, black in color except the tail, which is brown and resembles the braided lash of a whip.

THE TURTLE-HEAD.

The Turtle-head is very similar to the bull-snake.

THE STINGING-SNAKE.

The stinging-snake is a glossy black; never gets very large; is found in the swamps of the South in damp places and stings with his tail the same as a bee.

THE HORN-SNAKE.

The horn-snake, sometimes called the hoop-snake has a sharp horn on the end of his tail which he uses to defend himself with, but I have never seen them roll.

THE PINE-SNAKE.

The pine-snake is a large pieded snake, found in the Northern States and in British America.

THE BOA CONSTRICTOR.

The Boa Constrictor is the largest species of snake in the world and are found in Africa.

THE ANACONDA.

The Anaconda, next to the largest specie in the world; they are found in South America, and marked very much like the bull-snake.

THE PRAIRIE-RACER.

The Prairie-racer is grey in color, found on the Southern prairies.

Antidote for Snake Bites.

THE following are some of the antidotes I have obtained from different people who claimed they had used them with success.

Tried by a man in Portland, Oregon. "Apply immediately to the wound a poltice of indigo (or common washing bluing), and salt in equal parts, mixed with cold water, and renew every two or three hours, not forgetting to tie a ligature very tightly (or it is perfectly useless), above and below the wound to stop the spread of the poison in the veins, and drink freely of whiskey.—CHARLES A. SPAULDING, Portland, Oregon.

Tried by a man in South Carolina. "Onion, if applied immediately will draw out the poison, and it is about as easily cured as a bee sting and should be treated about the same, only with more promptness. Cut the onion in two crosswise (not lengthwise), hold a part of the onion on the wound for five minutes, when it will turn green, remove it and apply the other half and let it remain on about the same time. It will take two or three onions to effect a cure. If the person has been bitten, say half or three-quarters of an hour, you must apply nitrate of silver to the wound and take plenty of whiskey inwardly.—MR. HENRY DEAN, Charleston, South Carolina.

In the Cape of Good Hope, South Africa, where there are so many deadly serpents, many people are bitten every year, often fatally. Cobra de Capello's and puff-adders are two of the commonest snakes all over the colony. A clergyman who resided where the puff-adders swarm had been very successful among his people in his treatment of their bites, and for the benefit of the whole colony he published his recipe.

He writes:—

The following is the best mode of using this invaluable antidote: Mix a teaspoonful of ipecacuanha powder with a little cold water, then scarify the part bitten making two or three cuts through the skin and apply the same as a poultice. This should be followed by about thirty grains in a wine-glass full of cold water as an emetic, and, if necessary, both may be repeated in half an hour. This is seldom required to complete the cure, as the pain generally ceases in less than that time, and appetite and health speedily follow.

In some of the fine agricultural districts of South Africa, the wheat fields abound with puff-adders. Formerly, when engaging the reapers—mostly Hottentots—they would rarely consent to begin work without a "Snake Doctor" to accompany them to the fields. All Hottentots are great smokers, but the "doctor" delights in short black pipes, never cleaned and so pregnated with nicotine; no white man could use them. He generally amuses himself hunting the reptiles for a while, then smokes and takes a nap till wanted.

Should a reaper be bitten, the old fellow rouses up at once, as he knows quick work is everything in a snake bite, and his reputation is at stake, too. He applies a ligature above and below the wound, if possible, tightening to strangulation of the parts, a drop of nicotine is extracted from his pipe, and after well scarifying the wound, it is rubbed in. Another drop is diluted and put in the patient's mouth, followed by continuous draughts of firy "brandwein" or Cape brandy, when he is carried home, and according to the constitution of the man in the length of time he takes to recover.

Special Notice to the Public.

Since Clark Stanley has been advertising SNAKE OIL LINIMENT in the Eastern States, there has been a number of poor imitations sold by canvassing agents and street fakirs. Some going so far as to claim that they are agents of Clark Stanley.

Clark Stanley has no travelling agents. The Snake Oil Liniment is sold through the druggists only.

Below are a few names of the imitations of Clark Stanley's Snake Oil Liniment:

Snake Oil, Snake Liniment, Rattle Snake Liniment and similar names.

The genuine Clark Stanley's Snake Oil Liniment is made from a combination of oils. The principle oil being Rattle Snake Oil.

When buying Snake Oil Liniment, see that the name **CLARK STANLEY'S SNAKE OIL LINIMENT** is blown in the bottle. Don't be deceived by travelling agents and so-called street fakirs who offer for sale any of the above-named imitations. No reputable druggist will handle any of the above-named worthless imitations if they have heard of Clark Stanley's Snake Oil Liniment.

CLARK STANLEY.

CLARK STANLEY'S
Snake Oil Liniment,
GOOD FOR MAN AND BEAST.

Vastly superior to every other Liniment known.

A wonderful Pain Destroying Compound.

A SMALL QUANTITY OF
CLARK STANLEY'S
Snake Oil Liniment

with propper rubbing will Limber and Restore Stiff Joints. Use it in all cases of RHEUMATISM and INFLAMMATIONS, it Cools, Softens, Relaxes, Subdues. It is absorbed and serves to stimulate and harden the Tissues, equalizing the circulation.

PRICE, 50 CENTS PER BOTTLE.
FOR SALE BY ALL DRUGGISTS.

Clark Stanley's Snake Oil Liniment is used by the Western stock raisers. It is the best Liniment known for the cure of Sprains, Strains, Stiff Joints and Soreness in Muscles. For a horse that is stiff and sore after a long and hard drive, the limbs and chest should be rubbed well with the Liniment. It cures.

Deformities of the Human Hand from a Rheumatic Affliction.

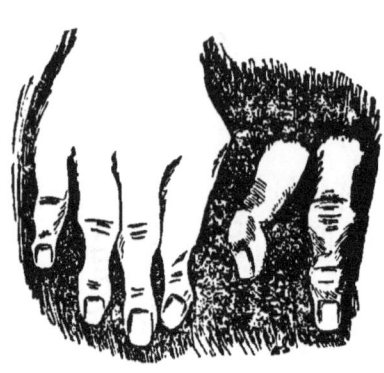

FINGERS OF A YOUNG GIRL DISTORTED BY THE DISEASE.

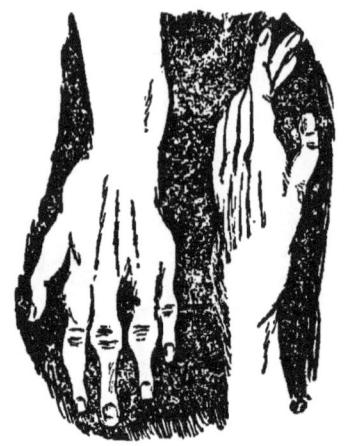

SWELLING OF JOINTS AND WRIST

FINGER ENDS BENT AND FIXED.

THE EFFECT OF GOUT.

SNAKE OIL LINIMENT

is a wonderful remedy. It will reduce enlarged joints to their natural size and will cure pain or lameness.

When your joints are stiff and your muscles sore from strain or rheumatism

SNAKE OIL LINIMENT
SHOULD BE USED FREELY.

The great liniment. When you have a bodily ache or pain of any nature, rub in a little Snake Oil Liniment, and it will fix you all right. The next morning you'll never know you were afflicted.

SEE CUTS FOR SCIENTIFIC MANNER IN WHICH TO APPLY
Clark Stanley's Snake Oil Liniment.

Fig. 1. Muscular Rheumatism.

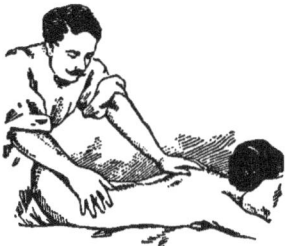

Fig. 2. Muscular Rheumatism.

Figures 1 and 2. For Muscular Rheumatism **or Pains in the Back, always rub** towards the Hips.

Fig. 3. Weakness or Pain in the Shoulders and Spine.

Fig 10. Headache.

Fig. 3. Pains and Weakness extending from the base of the brain the entire length of the spine. Stand the Patient as in the illustration, and with the balls of the fingers bathe and rub Clark Stanley's Snake Oil Liniment well into the spinal colum. Always rub down. Use the treatment twice in twenty-four hours, upon arising in the morning and retiring at night.

Figure 10 illustrates the way to bathe the head for Neuralgia, Headache, Tic Douloureux. Use Clark Stanley's Snake Oil Liniment freely and the pain will leave instantly. Bathe the head from temple to temple.

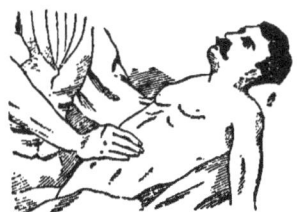

Fig. 13. Indigestion.

Fig 14. Indigestion

Figures 13 and 14 illustrate how you should use Clark Stanley's Snake Oil Liniment for Chest Pains, downward rubbing will effect immediate relief.

For Sale by all Druggists.   *PRICE, 50c. PER BOTTLE.*

CLARK STANLEY'S SNAKE OIL LINIMENT
THE GREAT EXTERNAL REMEDY FOR ALL ACHES AND PAINS.

Fig. 17. Partial Paralysis.

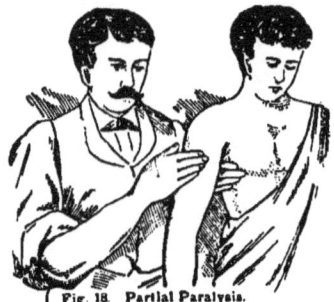

Fig. 18. Partial Paralysis.

Figures 17 and 18 illustrate the best method of curing **Partial** Paralysis of the Arms; the same rule applying to the lower limbs. For Paralysis, the rubbing is up and down, in all and every direction. Clark Stanley's Snak Oil Liniment is the only known remedy that will cure Paralysis. The rubbing and friction must be persevered in as often as the skin will stand the irritation.

Fig. 5. Lumbago.

Fig. 6. Lumbago.

Figures **5** and **6** show the position of the **patient suffering with** Lumbago. Clark Stanley's Snake Oil Liniment should be applied freely.

Fig. 20. Neuralgia.

Fig. 21. Loss of Muscular Power.

Figure 20 illustrates the best manner of applying Clark Stanley's Snake Oil Liniment for Pains in the back of the Head and Neck. These pains are of Neuralgic origin.

Figure 21 represents the manner of applying Clark Stanley's Snake Oil Liniment for Muscular **Weakness**. Rub towards the body.

Clark Stanley's
SNAKE OIL LINIMENT

THE GREAT EXTERNAL REMEDY FOR ALL ACHES AND PAINS.

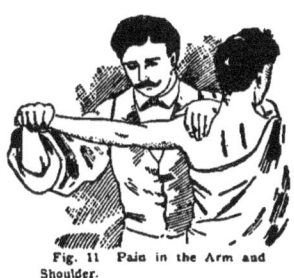

Fig. 11   Pain in the Arm and Shoulder.

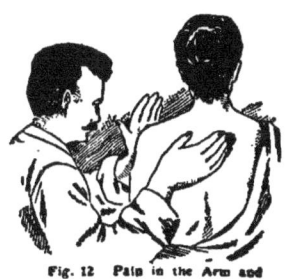

Fig. 12   Pain in the Arm and Sholder.

Figures 11 and 12 show the way to use Clark Stanley's Snake Oil Liniment for Pains in the Arms and Shoulders.   Rub the arm towards the shoulder, and rub the shoulder towards the waist.

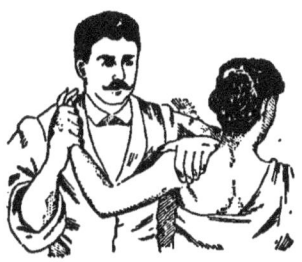

Fig. 15.   Contracted Cords.

Fig. 16.   Contracted Cords.

Figures 15 and 16 represent the correct manner to use Clark Stanley's Snake Oil Liniment for Contracted Cords, Stiff Joints, etc.   Rub the arm towards the body. Sometimes more than one application is necessary.

CLARK STANLEY'S SNAKE OIL LINIMENT cures with entire satisfaction, surely and promptly, all forms of Aches and Pains such as Rheumatism, Neuralgia, Lumbago, Backache, Headache, Toothache, Sore Throat, Swellings, Frostbites, Sprains and Bruises. It promises only what it can do under proof and does all it promises to do in the cure of pain.

Sold by all Druggists and Dealers everywhere.

PRICE, 50 CENTS PER BOTTLE.

CLARK STANLEY'S SNAKE OIL LINIMENT.

The most remarkable curative discovery ever made in any age or country. A Liniment that penetrates muscle, membrane and tissue to the very bone.

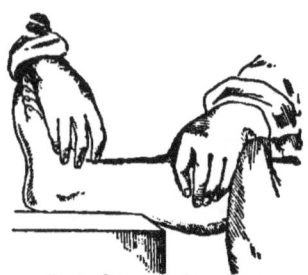

Fig. 7. Sciatica, or Rheumatism of the Legs.

BEFORE USING.

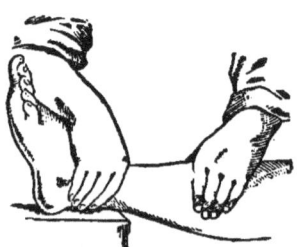

Fig. 8. Sciatica, or Rheumatism of the Legs.

AFTER USING.

Fig. 9. Sciatica. or Rheumatism of the Legs.

Figs. 7, 8 and 9 represents the correct way of applying Clark Stanley's Snake Oil Liniment for Sciatica or Rheumatism of the legs and joints. In all cases much depends upon the manner of rubbing the medicine in. Always rub down.

CLARK STANLEY'S SNAKE OIL LINIMENT,

For Sale by all Druggists.   PRICE, 50 CENTS PER BOTTLE.

IT CURES PAIN.

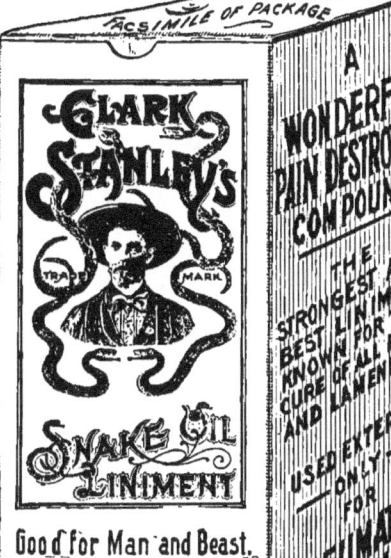

Clark Stanley's
SNAKE OIL LINIMENT

Comes in Manilla Colored Cartoon with name

CLARK STANLEY

Blown in every Bottle.

CLARK STANLEY'S
SNAKE OIL
LINIMENT

> sells fast for it is the best Liniment known for the cure of pain and lameness.

CLARK STANLEY'S
SNAKE OIL
LINIMENT

> will not freeze or get hard. It stands any climate.

CLARK STANLEY'S

Snake Oil Liniment

Does all it is advertised to do.

When you order Snake Oil Liniment don't forget the name

Clark Stanley.

Tell your druggist you want a bottle of Snake Oil Liniment. If he says he hasn't got it in stock, you tell him he can get it for you of any jobber in New England. It is the duty of every druggist to sell Snake Oil Liniment because it cures. Everybody knows enough things are sold that don't cure.

CLARK STANLEY'S SNAKE OIL LINIMENT
Cures Lumbago

You have heard about Lumbago "cures" before. You tried them, and you've still got Lumbago. Now, remember that SNAKE OIL LINIMENT is a totally different liniment from any other. It contains new and powerful ingredients that go through the pores and get at the real seat of pain. It cures cases of Lumbago that have defied all doctors and all other remedies. SNAKE OIL LINIMENT stops the hurting of all bodily aches and pains.

Many diseases require external, not internal treatment. Medicines that you swallow for

Rheumatism, Neuralgia, Lumbago and Sciatica,

seriously derange the digestive organs. SNAKE OIL LINIMENT will go through the pores of the skin direct, and cure the pains without causing some other disease. Apply SNAKE OIL LINIMENT where the pain is, and that will end the hurting. Nothing like it was ever before sold in America.

SNAKE OIL LINIMENT acts upon pain as water acts upon fire— puts it out completely and permanently. There is as much difference between it and other liniments as there is between diamonds and window glass. It stops the hurting of all bodily aches and pains — Rheumatism, Lumbago, Cold in the Chest, Backache, Tired Limbs, Aching Muscles, Sprains and Swellings. When you buy a bottle, you are not paying for an experiment. You are investing in a certainty. It cures.

SNAKE OIL LINIMENT serves the same purpose upon the human body as lubricating oil serves upon machinery. The sooner you realize that your body is nothing but a machine of flesh, muscles and bones, and the sooner you keep it in running order with SNAKE OIL LINIMENT the better off you will be.

Families who aim to keep some reliable medicines in their homes for use in cases of ailments or accidents, such as tooth-ache, a pain in the side or chest, lame back, bruises, frost bites, chilblains, sprains and swellings, will find Clark Stanley's Snake Oil Liniment to be reliable and we believe unequalled for the purpose for which it is intended.

CLARK STANLEY'S SNAKE OIL LINIMENT.

Have pity on your poor, tired, sore, aching, itching, swoolen feet! Just think how you abuse them. You stuff them into tight shoes every morning, and all day long they support the weight of your body. Is it any wonder they hurt at night?

It is for old folks and young folks — for poor people and rich people — for everybody who has much walking or standing up to do.

For a hard corn or calous, apply night and morning for three days and then you will tell your neighbours when you hear them com-

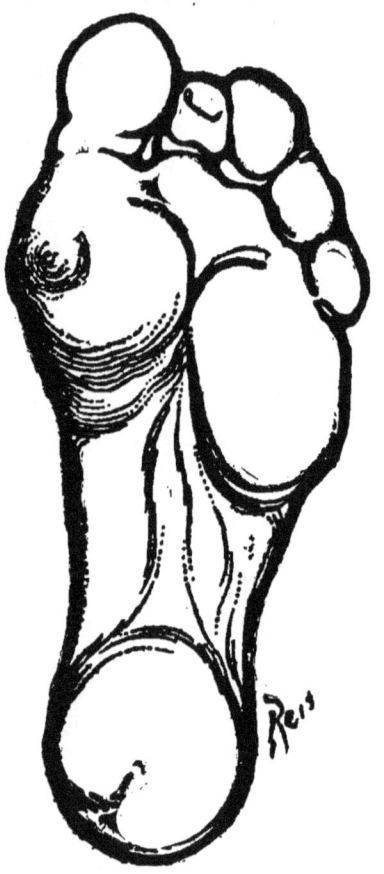

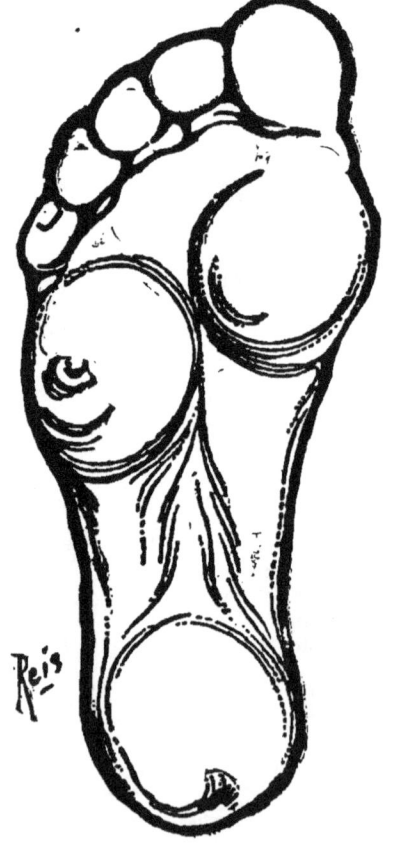

plain of their feet to go to the drug store and get a bottle of Clark Stanley's Snake Oil Liniment. It cures.

You don't need to suffer any more with your feet. There isn't a bit of use for it. Snake Oil Liniment will take out the soreness. It will stop the pain and itching. It will reduce the swelling. It will remove the tenderness, and make your feet just as good to walk on as they ever were. For Chilblains and Cold Feet it beats anything you ever saw or heard of.

Carpenters, blacksmiths and most all other mechanics frequently meet with slight accidents which cause them much annoyance and sometimes a loss of several days time. A strain or a sprain may be cured in one-third the time usually required by applying Clark Stanley's Snake Oil Liniment as soon as the injury is received. Try a bottle of Snake Oil Liniment.

Clark Stanley's
SNAKE OIL
LINIMENT
FOR
Old People

As people get old, their joints and muscles get stiff. They need a soothing, softening, relaxing oil to limber them up, and make their limbs supple like they were in younger days. The best thing for this is

SNAKE OIL LINIMENT.

It is a godsend to the aged if ever there was one. It makes the declining years of life free from the pains that come as the days go by. Many a grandfather and grandmother find SNAKE OIL LINIMENT the only thing that does their aches, pains and lameness any real good.

I do wish that more old people would read this advertisement of SNAKE OIL LINIMENT, and then go to the drug store and buy a bottle! Of course a great many folks don't believe SNAKE OIL LINIMENT is any good, but they'd think different after trying it. It really does do old people a lot of good. It cures rheumatism. It puts strength into weak backs, lame shoulders, and tired legs and arms. It takes stiffness out of the joints. It beats anything you ever saw. If old people will rub their stiff joints and aching bodies with SNAKE OIL LINIMENT every night upon re-

tiring, they'll feel much younger in the morning. It takes out the soreness and stiffness as nothing else ever did before. It loosens up the joints, cures lame arms and weak backs, and gives vigor and strength to the legs. It is for summer as much as winter use. It is for all pains and aches in flesh, muscles and joints.

Your druggist has it, or can get it for you if you demand it.

Clark Stanley's Snake Oil Liniment.

It is really astonishing how many people have trouble with their backs and shoulders. If the back is lame and weak, a person isn't much good for anything. You can't work or you can't enjoy yourself in any way. There is no use in having a weak back. Rub Snake Oil Liniment into it morning and night, and you will straighten right up.

www.ingramcontent.com/pod-product-compliance
Lightning Source LLC
Chambersburg PA
CBHW020253090426
42735CB00010B/1899